PAPER CREATIONS

CHRISTMAS ORIGAMI

DUY NGUYEN &
SOONBOKE SMITH

Main Street
A division of Sterling Publishing Co., Inc.
New York

2 4 6 8 10 9 7 5 3

Published by Sterling Publishing Co., Inc.
387 Park Avenue South, New York, NY 10016

© 2006 by Sterling Publishing Co., Inc.

This book is comprised of material from the following Sterling Publishing Co., Inc. titles:
Origami Holidays © 2002 by Duy Nguyen
Origami for the First Time® © 2003 by Soonboke Smith

Distributed in Canada by Sterling Publishing
c/o Canadian Manda Group, 165 Dufferin Street
Toronto, Ontario, Canada M6K 3H6
Distributed in the United Kingdom by GMC Distribution Services
Castle Place, 166 High Street, Lewes, East Sussex, England BN7 1XU
Distributed in Australia by Capricorn Link (Australia) Pty. Ltd.
P.O. Box 704, Windsor, NSW 2756, Australia

Printed in China
All rights reserved

Sterling ISBN-13: 978-1-4027-4006-0
ISBN-10: 1-4027-4006-9

For information about custom editions, special sales, premium and
corporate purchases, please contact Sterling Special Sales
Department at 800-805-5489 or specialsales@sterlingpub.com.

CONTENTS

BASIC INSTRUCTIONS

PAPER

The best paper to use for origami will be very thin, keep a crease well, and fold flat. It can be plain white paper, solid-color paper, or wrapping paper with a design only on one side. Regular typing paper may be too heavy to allow the many tight folds needed for some figures. Be aware, too, that some kinds of paper may stretch slightly, either in length or in width, and this may cause a problem in paper folding. Packets of paper especially for use in origami are available from craft and hobby shops.

Unless otherwise indicated, the usual paper used in creating these forms is square, 15 by 15 centimeters or approximately 6 by 6 inches. Some forms may call for half a square, *i.e.*, 3 by 6 inches or, cut diagonally, a triangle. A few origami forms require a more rectangular (legal) size or a longer piece of paper. For those who are learning and have a problem getting their fingers to work tight folds, larger sizes of paper can be used. Actually, any size paper squares can be used—slightly larger figures are easier to make than overly small ones. The paper provided within this gift set is 6 by 6 inches, easy to work with for origami novices.

GLUE

Use a good, easy-flowing but not loose paper glue, but use it sparingly. You don't want to soak the paper. A toothpick makes a good applicator. Allow the glued form time to dry. Avoid using stick glue, as the application pressure needed (especially if the stick has become dry) can damage your figure.

TECHNIQUE

Fold with care. Position the paper, especially at corners, precisely and see that edges line up before creasing a fold. Once you are sure of the fold, use a fingernail to make a clean, flat crease. Don't get discouraged with your first efforts. In time, what your mind can create, your fingers can fashion.

SYMBOLS & LINES

FOLD LINES

.... — - — - — - — — +++++++++++++++++

valley   mountain   Cut line

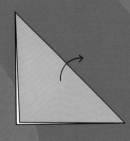

Turn over   Fold then unfold   Pleat fold   Crease line
or rotate   (repeated folding)

SQUARING
OFF PAPER

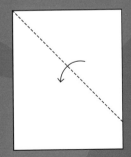
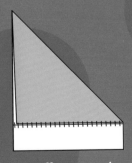

1. Take rectangular sheet,   2. Cut off excess on long   3. Unfold. Sheet is square,
valley fold diagonally.   side as shown.   ready for any size form.

BASIC FOLDS

KITE FOLD

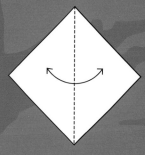 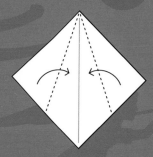 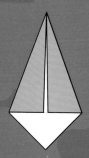

1. Fold and unfold a square diagonally, making a center crease.

2. Fold both sides in to the center crease.

3. This is a kite fold.

VALLEY FOLD

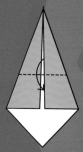

1. Here, using the kite, fold form toward you (forward), making a "valley."

2. This fold forward is a valley fold.

MOUNTAIN FOLD

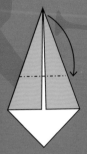

1. Here, using the kite, fold form away from you (backwards), making a "mountain."

2. This fold backwards is a mountain fold.

INSIDE REVERSE FOLD

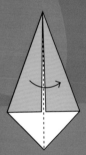

1. Starting here with a kite, valley fold kite closed.

2. Valley fold as marked to crease, then unfold.

3. Pull tip in direction of arrow.

4. Appearance before completion.

5. You've made an inside reverse fold.

OUTSIDE REVERSE FOLD

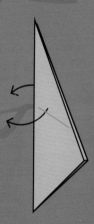

1. Using closed kite, valley fold, unfold.

2. Fold inside out, as shown by arrows.

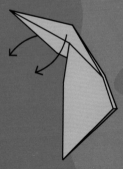

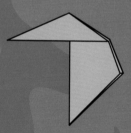

3. Appearance before completion.

4. You've made an outside reverse fold.

PLEAT FOLD

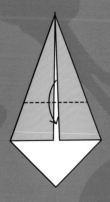 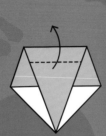 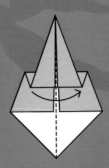 

1. Here, using the kite, valley fold.

2. Valley fold back again.

3. This is a pleat. Valley fold in half.

4. You've made a pleat fold.

PLEAT FOLD REVERSE

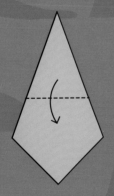 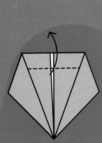 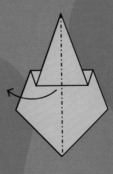 

1. Here, using the kite fold backwards, valley fold.

2. Valley fold back again for pleat.

3. Mountain fold form in half.

4. This is a pleat fold reverse.

SQUASH
FOLD I

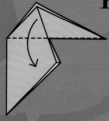

1. Using inside reverse, valley fold one side.

2. This is a squash fold I.

SQUASH
FOLD II

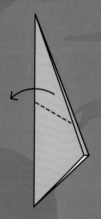

1. Using closed kite fold, valley fold.

2. Open in direction of the arrow.

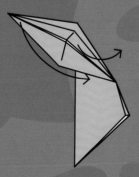

3. Appearance before completion.

4. You've made a squash fold II.

INSIDE CRIMP FOLD

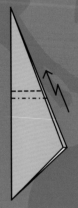 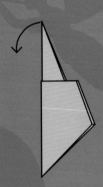 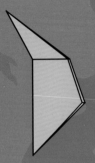

1. Here using closed kite fold, pleat fold.

2. Pull tip in direction of the arrow.

3. This is an inside crimp fold.

OUTSIDE CRIMP FOLD

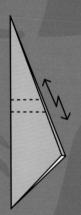 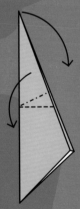 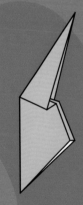

1. Here using closed kite fold, pleat fold and unfold.

2. Fold mountain and valley as shown, both sides.

3. This is an outside crimp fold.

BASIC FORMS

BASIC FORM I

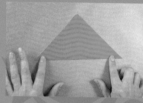  

1. Begin with a square. Fold and unfold in half diagonally in both directions (wrong side of paper is inside).

2. Rotate and fold in half (right side of paper is inside).

3. Unfold. Rotate and fold in half in other direction (right side of paper is inside).

4. Unfold. Turn model over. Collapse two opposite sides to the center along the horizontal fold.

5. Flatten model. Completed Basic Form I.

BASIC FORM II

1. Begin with a square. Fold in half (wrong side of paper is inside).

2. Unfold. Rotate and fold in half in other direction.

3. Unfold. Turn model over. Fold in half diagonally (right side of paper is inside).

4. Unfold. Fold in half diagonally in other direction (right side of paper is inside).

5. Unfold. Turn model over.

6. Fold two opposite side corners to meet at center.

7. Flatten model. Completed Basic Form II.

BASIC FORM III

1. Begin with the Basic Form II.

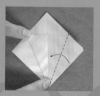

2. With opening at the bottom, fold bottom left side of upper flap to vertical midline.

3. Fold bottom right side of upper flap to vertical midline.

4. Rotate and fold folded corner of Square Base up to the center.

5. Unfold last three folds.

6. Rotate model and begin to form the upper wing by opening the upper flap at the bottom point, pulling it up as far as possible.

7. Press at left and right flap corners so the edges meet at the midline.

8. This will form a diamond. Turn the model over. Repeat Steps 2–7.

9. Completed Basic Form III.

BASIC FORM IV

1. Begin with the kite fold.

2. Rotate model and fold in half, bringing bottom corner to meet top corner.

3. Unfold last fold. Rotate model and fold bottom left side to horizontal midline.

4. Rotate model and fold bottom right side to horizontal midline.

5. Unfold the last two folds.

6. Lift corner A and then pull it downward so the side point moves toward the horizontal midline.

7. Rotate model. Lift corner B and then pull it downward so the side point moves toward the horizontal midline.

8. Completed Basic Form IV.

TRICOLOR
GIFT BOX

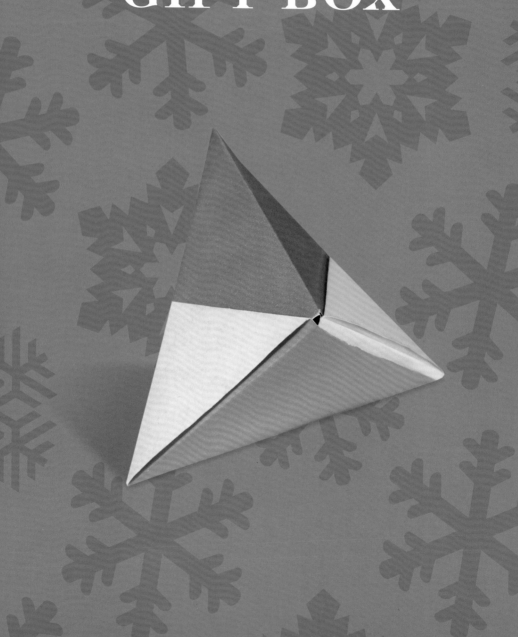

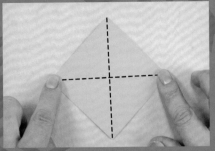

1. Begin with a square. Fold in half diagonally in both directions (wrong side of the paper is inside).

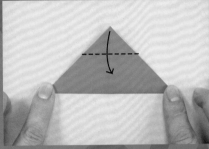

2. Fold upper top corner down to bottom, creating a flap.

3. Turn model over.

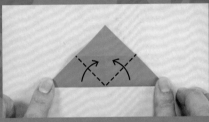

4. Fold left and right corners along dashed lines to meet at top corner.

5. Repeat Steps 1–4 with two contrasting colored pieces of paper to make three models.

6. Position the points of one model opposite the flap of another model.

7. Slide points of the one model under the flap of the other.

Note: The model will look like this after assembling the two pieces.

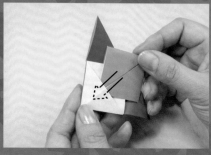

8. Repeat Steps 6–7, sliding points of remaining model under flap of second model.

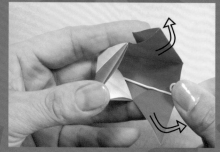

9. Pull points of first model outward, separating them.

10. Bring corner of third model toward center of first model.

11. Tuck points of first model under flap of third model.

12. Completed Tricolor Gift Box.

GIFT
BOX

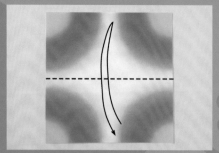

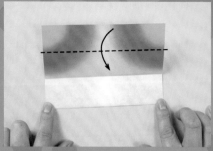

1. Begin with a square. Fold in half (right side of paper is inside). Unfold.

2. Fold bottom edge to the horizontal midline. Fold top edge to the horizontal midline.

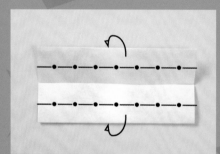

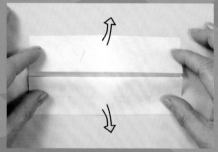

3. Turn model over. Fold top and bottom edges to horizontal midline, pulling flaps out from behind.

4. Completed Step 3.

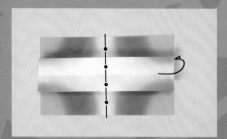

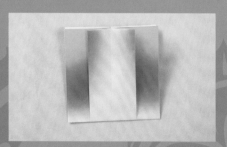

5. Rotate model and fold in half (wrong side of paper is inside).

6. Unfold last fold.

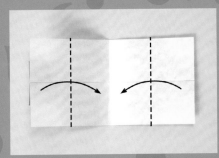

7. Fold top and bottom edges to horizontal midline.

8. Completed Step 7.

9. Rotate model. Unfold the last two folds.

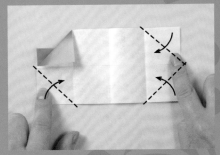

10. Fold top-left corner to the horizontal midline.

11. Fold remaining corners to horizontal midline, creating two tab ends.

12. Turn model over. Repeat Steps 1–11 to make six models.

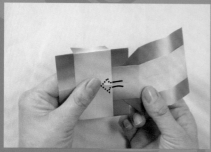

13. Insert one tab end of one model into the side of another.

Note: To help secure the assembly, apply glue to the end before inserting it into the side of other model.

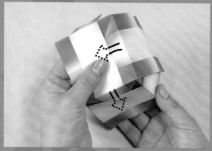

14. Continue inserting tab ends into sides of consecutive models to form a cube.

15. Insert a small gift before inserting the last tab end into the side of the next model. Do not glue last tab.

16. Completed Gift Box.

PICTURE FRAME

1. Begin with a square. Fold in half diagonally in both directions (wrong side of paper is inside).

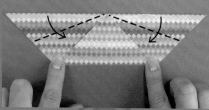

2. Rotate model. Fold bottom corner up to top edge. Fold left and right corners downward so top edges meet left and right edges of folded-up bottom corner.

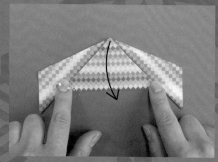

3. Unfold upper center flap.

4. Completed Step 3.

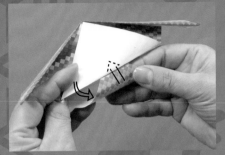

5. Tuck this flap inside the model. Unfold remaining center flap and tuck it inside the model.

6. Repeat Steps 1–5 to make four models.

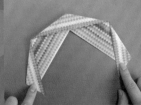

7. Apply glue to the right point of one model and slide it inside the left point of another model.

8. Repeat Step 7, gluing and sliding the remaining point inside the opposite point of the next model, until you have assembled a square.

9. Completed Picture Frame. Secure photo onto back of frame with glue. To hang on tree, pierce small hole in top of frame and thread string through.

SWAN BOX

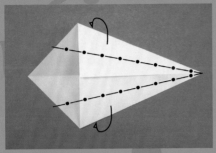

1. Begin with a kite fold. Turn model over. Fold top and bottom corners to horizontal midline.

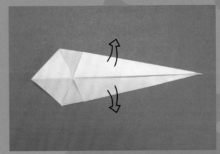

2. Pull flaps out from behind.

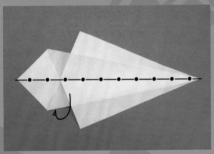

3. Fold in half (to the back) along horizontal midline.

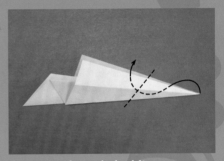

4. Crease along dashed line.

5. Reverse-fold by opening the model and collapsing the tip to the inside, keeping the center fold at the center.

6. Completed Step 5.

7. Fold along dashed line.

8. Tuck corner under top wing. Crease upper and lower flaps along dashed line of picture 9.

9. Reverse-fold by opening each flap and collapsing each tip to the inside.

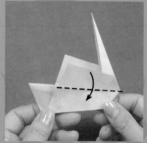

10. Fold each wing downward so top edge meets bottom fold.

11. Crease neck along dashed line.

12. Reverse-fold by opening the neck and collapsing the tip to the inside.

13. Push the tail toward the inside of the model.

14. Completed Swan Box.

PINE
TREE

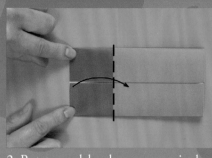

1. Trim brown origami paper into a 2" x 6" rectangle. Position the brown piece of paper on top of one side edge of the green paper. Glue the two pieces of paper together so you can begin with a square.

2. Rotate model so brown paper is along bottom edge. Fold in half vertically (wrong side of paper is inside). Unfold. Fold left and right sides to vertical midline. Fold bottom edge one-third of the distance toward top edge.

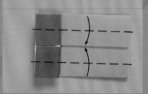

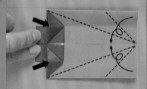

3. Fold the top two-thirds of resulting layer down.

4. Fold left and right sides to vertical midline.

5. Place your index finger between flaps on the bottom-left side and press to flatten. Repeat for bottom-right side. Fold top left and right corners to vertical midline.

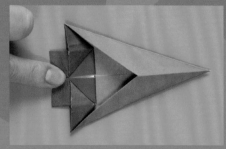

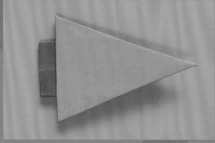

6. Fold top left and right corners again to vertical midline.

7. Turn model over. Completed Pine Tree. Punch along left and right slopes of tree. Wrap mini-string of lights around the tree as desired.

SNOWMAN

PART 1

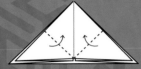 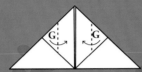 

1. Using Basic Form I, valley fold sides to center crease.

2. Apply glue (G) to triangles, then valley fold.

3. Make cuts to top layer as shown, and discard the two upper triangles.

4. Turn over to other side.

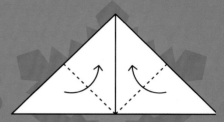

5. Again, valley folds to center crease.

6. Apply glue, then valley fold.

7. Make cuts to the top layer and discard triangles.

8. Blow into bottom center opening and pull form open, to inflate and form box.

9. Completed part 1, bottom body of snowman.

PARTS 2 & 3

1. For part 2, top body, make part 1 in smaller size.

2. For part 3, head, make part 1 in even smaller size.

TO ATTACH

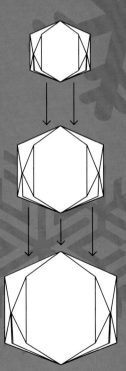

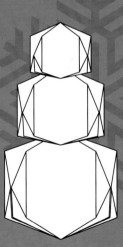

1. Build snowman, gluing bottom body, top body, and head together to hold.

2. Completed basic Snowman.

KRIS KRINGLE

PAPER USAGE

1 sheet 5.5" by 5.5" Part 1 (head)
1 sheet 2.25" by 2.25" Part 2 (face)
1 sheet 4. 25" by 4. 25" Part 3 (hat)
2 sheets 8.5" by 8.5" Part 4 (robe) & Part 5 (body)

PART 1

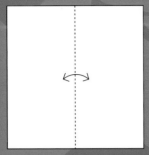

1. Valley fold then unfold.

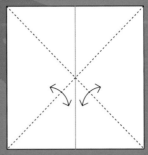

2. Valley folds then unfold.

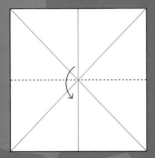

3. Valley fold.

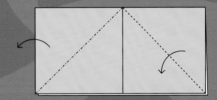

4. Mountain and valley fold.

5. Unfold both.

6. Squash fold.

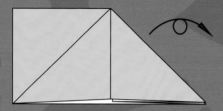

7. Turn over to other side.

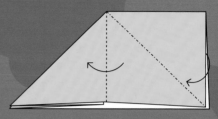

8. Squash fold.

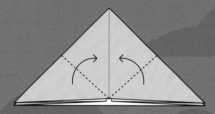

9. Valley folds.

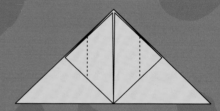

10. Valley folds.

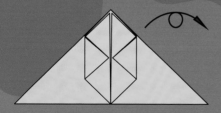

11. Turn over to other side.

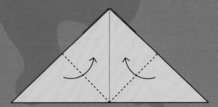

12. Valley folds.

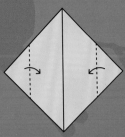

13. Valley folds.

14. Valley folds, front and back.

15. Valley and unfold, then tuck flaps into pockets as shown, front and back.

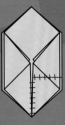

16. Cut through layers as shown.

17. Outside reverse fold, both sides.

18. Unfold both sides.

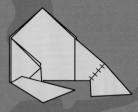

19. Cut through as shown.

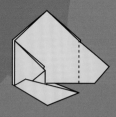

20. Valley fold and glue both sides to hold.

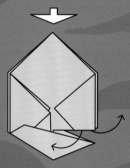

21. Push top down and open out.

22. Appearance before completion.

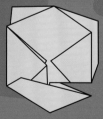

23. Completed part 1, Kris Kringle's head.

PART 2

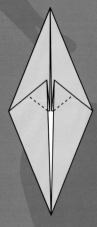

1. Start with Basic Form IV, then valley folds.

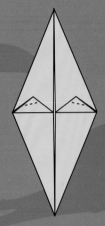

2. Inside reverse folds.

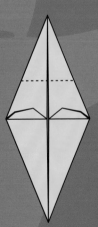

3. Valley fold.

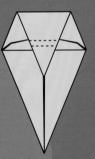

4. Pleat fold.

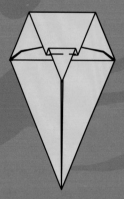

5. Valley fold.

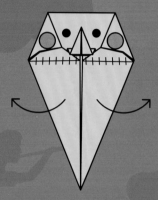

6. Draw eyes and cheeks, then cut and unfold.

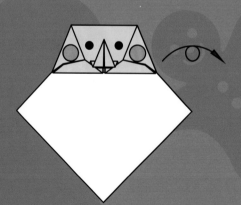

7. Turn over.

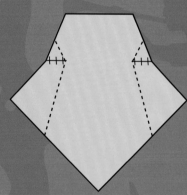

8. Cuts, then valley folds.

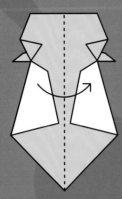

9. Valley fold in half.

10. Pull face outward slightly and squash fold.

11. Open out.

12. Completed part 2, Kris Kringle's face.

PART 3

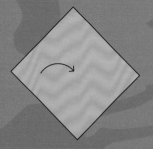

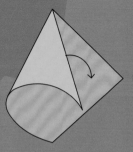

1. Roll corner of square sheet in direction of arrow.

2. Form into cone and glue to hold.

3. Cut as shown.

4. Valley folds.

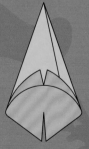

5. Cut as shown.

6. Completed part 3, Kris Kringle's hat.

PART 4

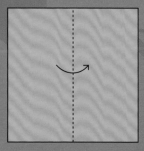

1. Valley fold in half.

2. Valley fold layers together and apply glue to hold.

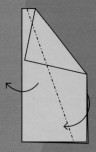

3. Open form and squash fold.

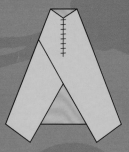

4. Cut top layer only, and return to previous position.

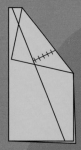

5. Cut through as shown.

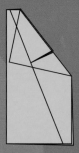

6. Squash fold open again.

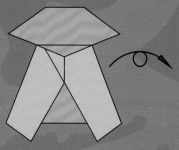

7. Turn over to other side.

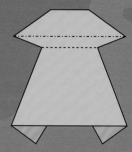

8. Pleat fold.

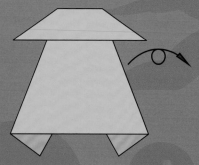

9. Turn over to other side.

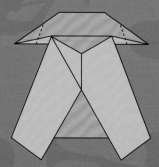

10. Valley folds, tucking flaps behind form.

11. Squash fold to side view.

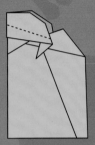

12. Outside reverse fold.

13. Inside reverse fold.

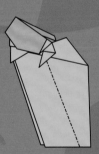

14. Squash fold to front view.

15. Completed part 4, Kris Kringle's robe.

PART 5

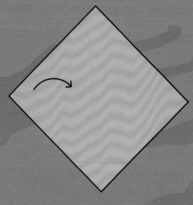

1. Roll square sheet in direction of arrow.

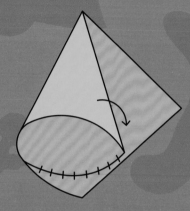

2. Form into cone, glue to hold. Cut off excess.

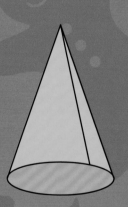

3. Completed part 5, Kris Kringle's body.

TO ATTACH

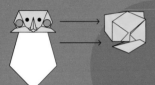

1. Join and glue head and face together as shown.

2. Add hat and glue to hold.

3. Completed head of Kris Kringle.

4. Join head, robe, and body together. Glue to hold.

5. Completed Kris Kringle.

SANTA CLAUS

PAPER USAGE

4 sheets 4. 25" by 4. 25" Part 1 (hat) & Part 3 (body liner) & Part 5 (two boots)
2 sheets 2.25" by 2.25" Part 1 (pompom) & Part 2 (face)
1 sheet 5.5" by 5.5" Part 2 (head)
2 sheets 8.5" by 11" Part 3 (robe) & Part 4 (legs)
3 strips 1.5" by 11" Parts 1 and 3 (white trim)
1 sheet 2" by 11" Part 6 (belt)
1 sheet 12.75" by 12.75" Part 7 (toy sack)

PART 1

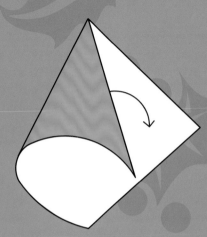

1. Roll square into cone, and glue.

2. Cut off excess.

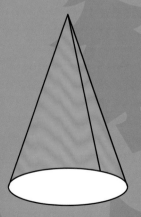

3. Top part of hat.

4. Start with paper strip, valley fold.

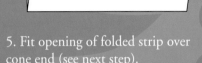

5. Fit opening of folded strip over cone end (see next step).

6. Wrap completely around cone end. Apply glue as you go.

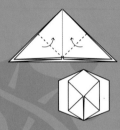

7. Form pompom in small size (see Snowman pages 31–32).

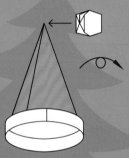

8. Glue pompom to one side of tip of hat. Rotate.

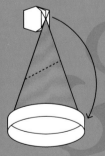

9. Valley fold to one side as shown, glue to hold pompom in position.

10. Completed part 1, Santa Claus's hat. (A large-size hat makes a cute decoration in itself!)

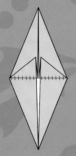

PART 2

1. Start with Basic Form IV, cut top layer only as shown.

2. Unfold left and right.

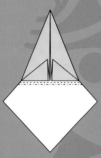

3. Pleat fold.

4. Cuts as shown.

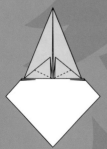

5. Valley folds.

6. Inside reverse folds.

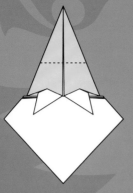

7. Valley fold.

8. Pleat fold.

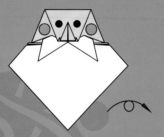

9. Add eyes, cheeks. Turn over.

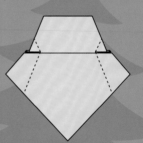

10. Valley folds.

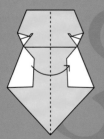

11. Valley fold in half.

12. Pull and crimp fold.

13. Valley unfold.

14. Tuck face section behind mustache.

15. Valley folds.

16. Completed face section, for head.

17. Make head from new square (see Kris Kringle, pages 35–38).

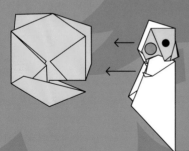

18. Attach Santa face to head.

19. Completed part 2, Santa's head.

PART 3

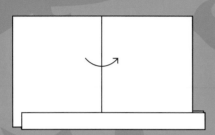

1. Valley fold strip to fit over sheet as shown, then valley fold in half.

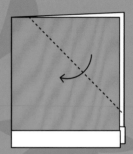

2. Valley fold both layers.

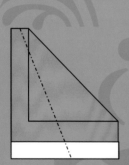

3. Glue and squash fold to open out front.

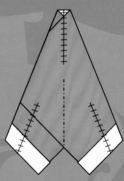

4. Cut as shown, then return to Step 3 position.

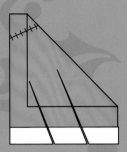

5. Cut off section as shown.

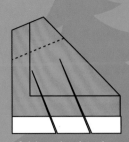

6. Valley fold on both sides.

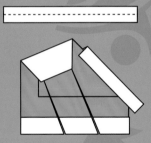

7. Trim strip length. Valley fold, then glue. Squash fold.

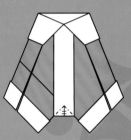

8. Cut and mountain folds.

9. Valley fold arm.

10. Valley fold other arm.

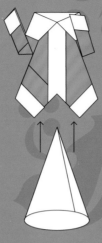

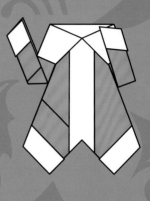

11. Roll a new sheet into cone. Glue and cut off excess.

12. Insert cone into Santa's robe for better stability. Glue to hold.

13. Completed part 3, Santa's body. (Liner hidden.)

PART 4

1. Roll rectangular sheet lengthwise into tube, and glue to hold.

2. Partially cut tube in center, then pull in direction of arrows.

3. Completed legs.

PART 5

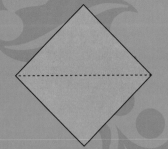

1. Valley fold.

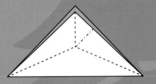

2. Pinch top layer together, then mountain fold as shown.

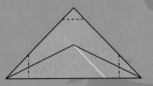

3. Mountain fold, then valley folds.

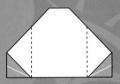

4. Valley folds.

5. Pull together as shown and glue to hold.

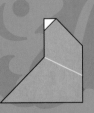

6. Completed part 5, Santa's boot. Now repeat (make 2).

PART 6

1. Strip of paper, valley fold in thirds.

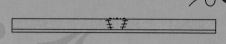

2. Cut top layer as shown, then mountain fold flap to reverse side. Turn over.

3. Completed part 6, Santa's belt.

PART 7

1. Start with Basic Form II. Valley fold.

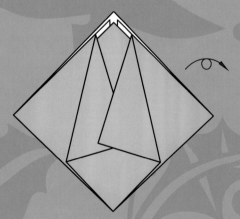

2. Apply glue, then turn over.

3. Valley folds and glue.

4. Valley fold both sides.

5. Valley fold both sides.

6. Valley fold both sides.

7. Push bottom upward and open top. (Open only one side when attaching to Santa.)

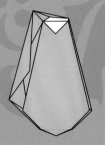

8. Completed part 7, Santa's toy sack.

TO ATTACH

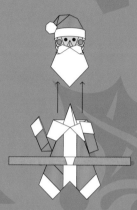

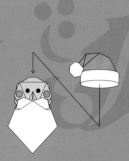

1. Attach hat to head.

2. Glue head onto body and add belt.

3. Glue sack onto shoulder, if wanted. Attach boots to legs and legs to body, in standing or sitting position.

4. Completed Santa Claus standing…and sitting.

REINDEER

PART I

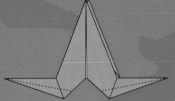

1. Start with Basic Form III. Inside reverse folds.

2. Valley folds on both sides.

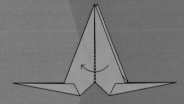

3. Valley fold in half. Rotate form.

4. Outside reverse fold.

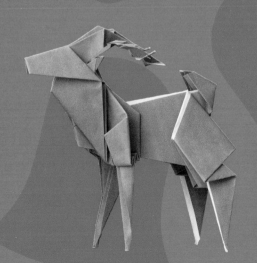

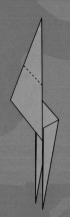

5. Outside reverse folds.

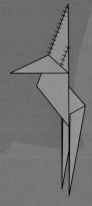

6. Make cuts as shown.

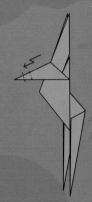

7. Pleat folds.

8. Outside reverse fold.

9. Pleat folds on both sides.

10. Tuck ears in.

11. Pleat folds.

12. Pull and crimp fold.

13. Inside reverse folds.

14. Mountain folds on both sides.

15. Cuts and valley folds.

16. Completed part 1, front of reindeer.

PART II

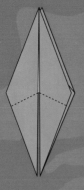

1. Start with Basic Form III. Valley folds.

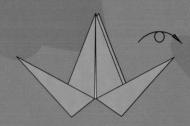

2. Turn over to other side.

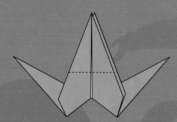

3. Valley fold.

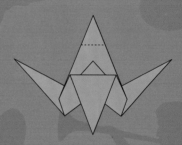

4. Valley fold.

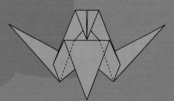

5. Valley folds.

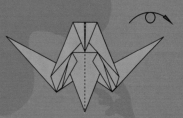

6. Fold in half, then rotate.

7. Outside reverse fold.

8. Make cut as shown. Inside reverse fold, both sides.

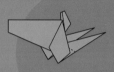

9. Inside reverse folds, both sides.

10. Completed part 2, rear of reindeer.

TO ATTACH

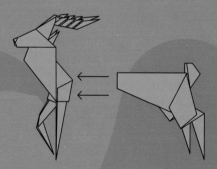

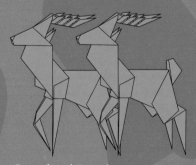

1. Join both parts together, and apply glue to hold.

2. Completed Reindeer.

SANTA'S SLEIGH

PART 1

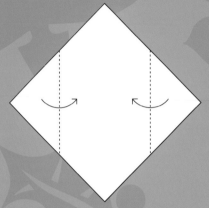 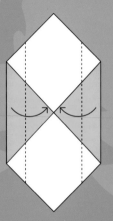

1. Valley folds to center.　2. Again, valley folds to center.

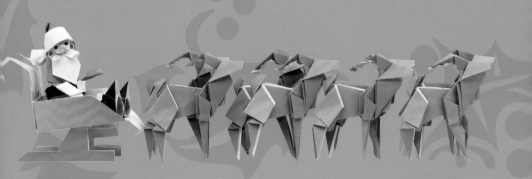

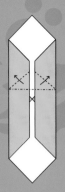

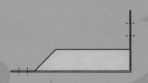

3. Valley/mountain folds to boxlike shape, glue to hold.

4. Side view, mountain folds.

5. Completed part 1, top of Santa's sleigh.

PART 2

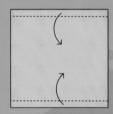

1. Valley folds.

2. Make cuts as shown.

3. Valley folds, right side then left.

4. Valley folds.

5. Mountain fold on both sides.

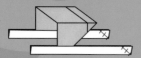

6. Make cuts as shown, and discard.

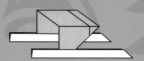

7. Completed part 2, runners of Santa's sleigh.

TO ATTACH

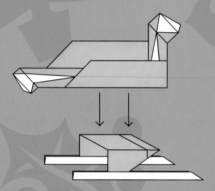

1. Join sleigh parts 1 and 2 together as shown and apply glue to hold.

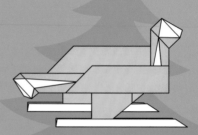

2. Completed Santa's Sleigh.

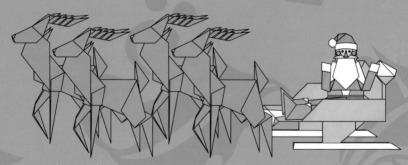

3. With reindeer and Santa added, ready to go!

ANGEL

PAPER USAGE

1 sheet 8.5" by 8.5" Part 1 (top body)
1 sheet 8.5" by 5" Part 2 (lower body)
1 sheet 2" by 6" Part 3 (hair)
1 sheet 4" by 12" Part 4 (wings)

PART 1

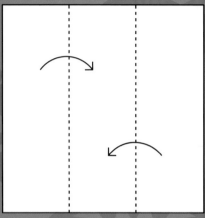

1. Valley fold sheet as shown, in thirds.

2. Apply glue to lower inside front layer only.

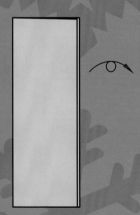

3. Turn over.

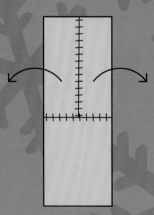

4. Cuts to top layer only, then open out to sides.

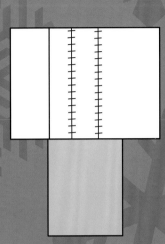

5. Make cuts as shown.

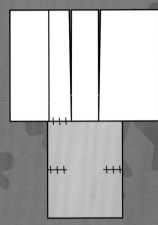

6. Cut and remove top strip. Make side cuts through.

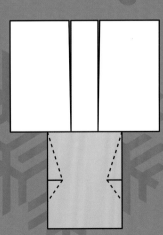

7. Valley fold side sections.

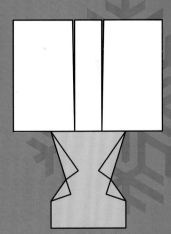

8. Apply glue to side folds.

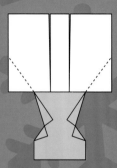

9. Valley folds.

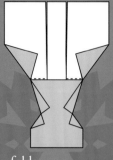

10. Valley folds.

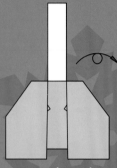

11. Turn over to other side.

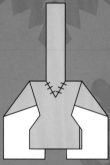

12. Cut front layer and discard.

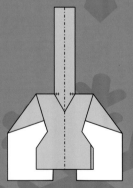

13. Cuts, then mountain fold.

14. Inside reverse fold.

15. Inside reverse fold.

16. Outside reverse fold.

17. Cut as shown.

18. Inside reverse fold, then glue closed.

19. Valley folds.

20. Cuts as shown.

21. Valley folds.

22. Mountain folds.

23. Mountain folds.

24. Glue hands together.

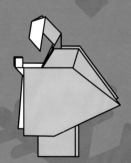

25. Completed part 1, top of angel.

PART 2

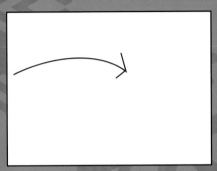

1. Roll into tube shape to fit inside angel top, and glue.

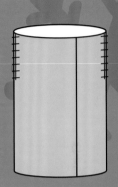

2. Cuts as shown.

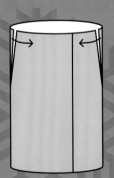

3. Taper both sides and glue.

4. Completed part 2, lower body of angel.

PART 3

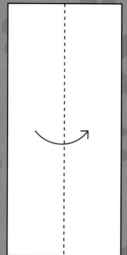

1. Valley fold strip.

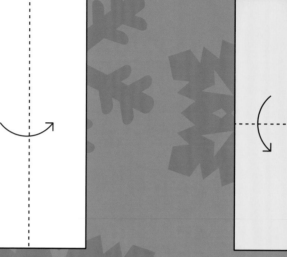

2. Valley fold.

3. Inside reverse fold.

4. Cut off as shown.

5. Completed part 3, hair of angel.

PART 4

1. Start with strip of paper, valley fold.

2. Valley fold, then rotate.

3. Valley fold.

4. Squash fold.

5. Mountain fold.

6. Cut as shown.

7. Valley fold both sides.

8. Valley fold both sides.

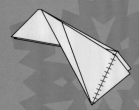

9. Cuts as shown.

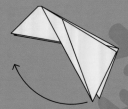

10. Unfold, to open out wings.

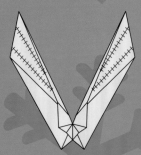

11. Make cuts.

12. Completed part 4, wings of angel.

TO ATTACH

1. Join hair to top of angel; glue to hold.

2. Valley fold arms open.

3. Back view, join wings to upper body and the upper body to lower body, and glue.

4. Back view of joined angel. Turn over.

5. Completed Angel.

INDEX